TOO MANY PETS

TOO MANY PETS

by Mark Anderson
Illustrations by Asa Crowe

Copyright © 2021 by Mark Anderson.

ISBN-978-1-6379-0895-2

All rights reserved. No part of this book may be reproduced or transmitted in any form or by any means, electronic or mechanical, including photocopying, recording, or by any information storage and retrieval system, without permission in writing from the copyright owner.

The views expressed in this work are solely those of the author and do not necessarily reflect the views of the publisher, and the publisher hereby disclaims any responsibility for them.

Matchstick Literary
1-888-306-8885
orders@matchliterary.com

Dedicated to Krista and all my friends at Sacred Space Yoga for their encouragement and for their willingness to serve as a captive audience while I read my poems.

Speak up, my dear,
are you trying to say
I have too many pets
and they get in the way?
Others have told me that,
you're not the first.
That's why my answer
is so well rehearsed.
If you're speaking of dogs,
I have only two,
a basset named Basil
and a boxer named Boo.
As for cats, I have several,
at least one, two, three,
Gaston and Mudpie
and Annabelle Lee.
Those three come with me
wherever I go.
There might be some more
in the barn, I don't know.

Too many pets? Don't make me laugh!
I only have one tiny, baby giraffe.
She helps with the yardwork, performing with ease,
at tending the lawn and pruning the trees.
At pruning a tree, she's much better than me
and that's why I keep her around, don't you see?

And they care of themselves.
At least some of them can.
Take, for example,
my orangutan.
He eats only oatmeal,
he cooks it himself,
and he keeps all his stuff
on his personal shelf.
He cooks it for breakfast
everyday,
then he washes his dishes
and puts them away.
He plays with my squirrels.
They're tree acrobats.
And at night he comes down
and he sleeps with the cats.

Don't freak out! A large spider is stuck in your hair!
For you, its probably your baddest nightmare!
But that's only Alice, so calm down, my dear.
She's really quite friendly, she lives with me here.
She spins a neat web in my kitchen nearby,
and when I have guests she comes out to say, "Hi".
She must have got lost, poor little waif.
Hold still, I'll remove her to where she'll be safe.

Too many pets?
I find that absurd.
Sometimes I think
I need some more birds.
I have a few peacocks
that roam here and there.
I feed lots of finches
but they live elsewhere.
I fill all my feeders
with sunflower seed,
they come at their leisure
and take what they need.
One feathered fellow
that lives in my zoo
is a gentleman owl
I call Dr. Whooo.
With wonderful manners
in conduct and speech,
a perfect example
for parents to teach.
He always says, "thank you"
or else, "if you please".
He gets along fine
with the chickens and geese!

Too many pets?
How could that be?
When my possums had babies
I only kept three!
The rest were adopted
by neighbors of mine,
and the last time checked
they were all doing fine.
They stay with my rabbits
in cages on shelves .
But my family of muskrats
take care of themselves.
They live in a burrow
way down by the creek
but they come by to visit
about once a week.
When I know they're coming
I cook up a pot
of cheese ravioli.
They like it a lot.

You may think it excessive to keep buffaloes
but up until Tuesday I didn't have those.
They arrived in the night in a terrible storm .
In my barn, found a place that was cozy and warm.
I made them hot chocolate and threw down some hay
and I'm happy to tell you they're planning to stay.
Their family was stuck in a terrible spot.
When they asked, "could we stay?"
I replied, "sure, why not?"

Too many pets, I say, *"au contraire!"*
There's plenty of space for my cinnamon bear.
He has his own room and he has his own cot.
Because during the winter he sleeps quite a lot.
With his comforter pulled right up to his neck,
you should come see him he's cuter than heck.

This life that I lead
is as good as it gets
In fact I've been thinking
of getting more pets.
I don't have a ferret,
I don't have a mink,
I don't have a skunk
that's been fixed
not to stink.
I visit each pet
every day when they feed
or when I bring round
other stuff that they need.
like blankets or pillows
or music or toys.
It's a full time job
and I'm always employed.
I always have something
to look forward toward.
And I never get lonely,
I never get bored

"Too many pets!" are three words I don't need to hear.
Come on, admit it, you're jealous, my dear!

www.ingramcontent.com/pod-product-compliance
Lightning Source LLC
Chambersburg PA
CBHW041108070526
44583CB00002B/112